GW01019281

A Book of Prayers
- for -
New Parents

This edition copyright © 1995 Lion Publishing
Illustrations copyright © 1995 William Geldart

Published by
Lion Publishing plc
Sandy Lane West, Oxford, England
ISBN 0 7459 3357 2
Albatross Books Pty Ltd
PO Box 320, Sutherland, NSW 2232, Australia
ISBN 0 7324 1319 2

First edition 1995
10 9 8 7 6 5 4 3 2 1

Acknowledgments
Illustrations by William Geldart

Prayer acknowledgments are on page 64.

A catalogue record for this book is available
from the British Library

Printed and bound in Singapore

A BOOK OF PRAYERS
- for -
New Parents

LION
Giftlines

Contents

Introduction

Children are a gift from the Lord;
they are a real blessing

FROM PSALM 127

The arrival of children is one of the most awe-inspiring, frightening, fantastic, life-changing experiences we can ever go through. It will certainly draw upon every reserve of strength, wisdom and faith that we possess – and then some! In fact, one of the many gifts children have is to remind us of our dependence upon others. As new parents we need other people – family and friends, a supportive community and trained professionals. We also need to draw upon the resources available to us through prayer.

This book will provide a constant resource in the next few years. Prayers for yourselves; words to capture a special moment; guidance for the beginnings of your baby's prayer life, from the earliest moments round the cot, to the family prayer time.

Babies learn what is important to you by watching what you do and the way you do it, long before they understand the words you say. As prayer together becomes a way of life, so your child will grow up in the confidence that he or she is known and loved by God.

Giving thanks

Welcome baby, special person,
Welcome to our world.
Like a leafbud, tightly folded,
Yet to be unfurled.
Fresh from sleeping,
fresh from dreaming,
Come from heaven above,
We to whom you have been given,
Bring you all our love.

Here you are then, a real, live human
being. After all that waiting, planning,
wondering, you're finally here. You make
our hearts swell with joy. Thank you, God,
for this very special moment.

God our Father, maker of all that is living, we praise you for the wonder and joy of creation. We thank you from our hearts for the life of this child, for a safe delivery, and for the privilege of parenthood. Accept our thanks and praise through Jesus Christ our Lord.

FROM THE ALTERNATIVE SERVICE BOOK 1980

For an adopted child

We receive this child into our family with
thanksgiving and joy. Through the love of
God we receive him/her; with the love of
God we will care for him/her; by the love
of God we will guide him/her; and in the
love of God may we all abide for ever.

FROM THE ALTERNATIVE SERVICE BOOK 1980

Not flesh of my flesh,
Not bone of my bone,
But still miraculously my own.
Never forget for a single minute
You didn't grow under my heart,
*   but in it.*

Baby's Name

You may like to use this little ceremony to make the giving of baby's name a special moment. It may involve just the two of you, or a small group of those closest to the family. Take the baby in your arms and say:

We give you the name

....

because

....

....

Each person holds the baby in turn and says:

Welcome *(name in full)*

....

to our family.

Lord Jesus Christ, whose name means
saviour and chosen one, bless this child,
named here, whom you have known from
the beginning.
May he/she grow up to know and
understand your name and to be named by
you in love.
Amen.

Prayers Around the Cot

It is never too early to begin a little prayer time with your baby. He or she will not understand the words you say, but will soon come to enjoy the quiet moment together.

In the morning

Jesus said: 'Let the children come to me.'
Then he took them in his arms, placed his
hands on each of them, and blessed them.

FROM MARK'S GOSPEL

Dear Lord here is.......................
bless him/her this day in every way.
God the Father, bless you;
God the Son, defend you;
God the Spirit, keep you this day
    and evermore.

At night

Goodnight.............. Sweet dreams.
God bless you as you sleep
and when you wake.

Dear Father, who lifts each sparrow,
holds each star in place,
bless and keep my baby in the palm of
    your hand
this night and every night.

God the Father, bless you;
God the Son, defend you;
God the Spirit, keep you this night
    and evermore.

Baby's Baptism

.... I baptize you in the name of
the Father, and of the Son, and of the Holy
Spirit. Amen.

Thank you, Father, that today our baby has
been signed with the sign of your cross.
May he/she not be ashamed to confess the
faith of Christ crucified and to fight
valiantly under his banner against sin, the
world and the devil. May he/she continue
Christ's faithful soldier and servant to the
end of his/her life.

Thank you Father for the candle we
received today. May our baby son/
daughter shine as a light in the world to
your glory.

Baby's Dedication

This is ....
We thank God for him/her.
We offer him/her back to God.
We pray for him/her and all his/her
   family.
We welcome him/her into this family of
   believers.

Father, we thank you that you have given us
families so that we can grow up surrounded
by love. Thank you, too that we belong to
the wider family of your church,
surrounding us with those who love and
serve you.

Prayers for New Parents

Thanksgiving

Lord Jesus Christ, we come to you with
our baby, we give this new life into your
care. As weakness turns into maturity,
may our child grow to love and trust you.
Lord Jesus, draw us together in deeper
love and understanding so that our child
may grow up in security and peace.

CHRISTIAN PUBLICITY ORGANIZATION

Watching them grow

Thank you, Father, for letting us care for this child, for the joy of watching him/her grow. Help us to provide the warmth, the love, and the security he/she needs now, so that when he/she stands alone, he/she will do so with courage and with confidence.

MARION STROUD

Worry

Lord, to look after a tiny child is such a responsibility. You know that sometimes we are at our wit's end. Help us to learn when we should worry and when we should not; when to cope alone and when to ask for help; when to pray and when to act. And as we learn on the job, grant us your help and your peace.

Responsibility

Lord, sometimes I am frightened by the
weight I feel to bring up these children that
you have entrusted to me . . . I know that I
will make mistakes, that I will fail my
children, that my strength and patience
will not be sufficient, that I will make the
wrong decisions, and that at times my love
will grow weak. Around me I see parents
labouring under the same weight, afraid in
the same way, trying their best. Help us all
to keep love going, and put your blessing on
our love which then has a chance to
overcome all the mistakes we will make.

ULRICH SCHAFFER

Wisdom

Father, give us wisdom as we care for this
child and bring him up for you. Don't let us
be so worried that we lose the happiness of
his early days and draw us closer together as
we discover the joys and pains of parenting.

On night-watch

Why is it, Lord God, that he seldom wants to sleep when we do? This child – he's like a human whirlwind in the daytime, and still wakes up at three in the morning to play. If he were ill or cold or hungry we could soothe him, but he's just bored, a little lonely, wide-awake. We've tried the remedies that they've suggested. We've put toys into his cot, a night-light in his room, fed him, watered him, picked him up, left him to cry . . . and still we keep night-watch while all around is wrapped in blissful, peaceful sleep. We need your help, dear God. Help us to be grateful for his glowing health, boundless energy and seemingly endless curiosity.

Give us the strength we need to face each new morning; clear thinking for the day's work; patience with the little problems that loom so large when we are tired, and wisdom so that we may know just how to meet his needs. And most of all help us to hang on to the assurance that, as with all of childhood's phases, this too will pass and one night we'll all enjoy some quiet, unbroken sleep.

MARION STROUD

Baby's First Birthday

Heavenly Father, how good you are! How
wonderful are your works.
We praise you for all your gifts.
Especially we thank you for your gift to
us of this dear child and for the year that
is past.

KATHARINE SHORT (ADAPTED)

One year has passed
since our baby first arrived
and changed our lives for ever.
Thank you, God, for every moment since
then and that today we are celebrating
   again.
We look back with wonder,
and forward with hope.
May the life just begun
be lived in the certainty of your love,
whatever comes.

First Prayers

Try to take a little time each day, as part of baby's routine, to establish a pattern of quiet and prayer. Long before they can understand, simply by what you do and the way you do it, young children learn what is important to you.

In the morning

Father, we thank you for the night,
And for the pleasant morning light;
For rest and food and loving care,
And all that makes the day so fair.

REBECCA F. WESTON

Thank you for the world so sweet,
Thank you for the food we eat.
Thank you for the birds that sing,
Thank you, God, for everything.

MRS E. RUTTER LEATHAM

At night

Jesus, tender Shepherd, hear me;
Bless your little lamb tonight;
Through the darkness please be near me;
Keep me safe till morning light.

MARY LUNDIE DUNCAN

Good night! Good night!
Far flies the light;
But still God's love
Shall flame above,
making all bright.
Good night! Good night!

VICTOR HUGO

First Graces

Thank you, Jesus,
for this food.
Amen.

For health and strength
and daily food
we praise your name
O Lord.

For every cup and plateful,
Lord make us truly grateful.

We thank you, Father, for your care
For all your children everywhere.
As you feed us all our days
May our lives be filled with praise.

Praise God from whom all blessings flow,
Praise him, all creatures here below,
Praise him above, you heavenly host,
Praise Father, Son and Holy Ghost.

Each time we eat,
may we remember God's love.

A PRAYER FROM CHINA

Milestones

Father thank you for every new discovery
our baby makes, and thank you for letting us
see your world anew, through his/her eyes.

Father,
a first smile,
first steps,
first words —
these are miracles of joy for parents.
This is what your joy must be
when we take our first, faltering steps
    towards you;
our first words of prayer;
and when we learn to smile back into your
smiling face.

Prayers with
pre-school children

*As your children become more used to family
routine, choose a convenient time for a few
prayers together. Mealtime is often the best.*

Thank you for each happy day,
For fun, for friends, and work and play;
Thank you for your loving care,
Here at home and everywhere.

For home and family

God bless all
those that I love;
God bless all those that love me.

FROM A NEW ENGLAND SAMPLER

May the love of God our Father
Be in all our homes today:
May the love of the Lord Jesus
Keep our hearts and minds always:
May his loving Holy Spirit
Guide and bless the ones I love,
Father, mother, brothers, sisters,
Keep them safely in his love.

FROM INFANT PRAYER

Bless this house which is our home
May we welcome all who come.

FROM HELLO GOD

For ourselves

Day by day, dear Lord, of thee three
    things I pray:
to see thee more clearly,
love thee more dearly,
follow thee more nearly,
day by day.

RICHARD OF CHICHESTER

Jesus, friend of little children,
Be a friend to me;
Take my hand and ever keep me
Close to thee.

WALTER JOHN MATHAUS

For friends

Bless my friends, Lord, and their friends,
And all their families too.
May they share the happiness,
That comes from loving you.

Thank you, God, for friends.
Thank you for fun and games and parties.
Thank you for my best friend.
Help me to be a good friend and keep my
     promises.
Help me to be friends even with those I
don't much like – because you love us all.

For the wide world

God, you made the world,
and you made us.
Show us how we should live.

To God who gives our daily bread
A thankful song we raise,
And pray that he who sends us food
May fill our hearts with praise.

THOMAS TALLIS

Going to playgroup

Thank you, God for my new playgroup.
I want to go again tomorrow. Goodnight.

A CHILD'S PRAYER

Father, bless playgroup today;
Be in all we do or say;
Be in every song we sing;
Every prayer to you we bring.

FROM LITTLE FOLDED HANDS

Prayers With Young Children

These prayers are for use with children from playgroup to infant school age.

About prayer

When I pray I speak to God,
when I listen God speaks to me.
I am now in his presence.
He is very near to me.

WORSHIP IN JUNIOR SCHOOLS

O make my heart so still, so still,
When I am deep in prayer,
That I might hear the white
    mist-wreaths
Losing themselves in air!

UTSONOMIYA SAN

God is always near me,
Hearing what I say
Knowing all my thoughts and deeds,
All my work and play.
    God is always near me,
Though so young and small;
Not a look or word or thought,
But God knows it all.

PHILIP BLISS

O Lord, open my eyes
to see what is beautiful;
My mind, to know what is true;
My heart, to love what is good:
for Jesus' sake.

The Lord's Prayer

Our Father
who art in heaven,
hallowed be thy name;
thy kingdom come;
thy will be done;
on earth as it is in heaven.
Give us this day our daily bread.
And forgive us our trespasses,
as we forgive those who trespass
    against us.
And lead us not into temptation;
but deliver us from evil.
For thine is the kingdom, the power,
and the glory, for ever and ever.
Amen.

A version for children

Our Father in heaven:
Your name is very special to us.
Be king of our hearts
so that we do what you want on earth
as they do in heaven.
Give us today the food we need.
Forgive us when we do wrong things,
and help us to forgive those who are
    unkind to us.
Please stop us from doing bad things,
and keep us safe from every danger.
Our hearts are yours.
You have all the power
and all the glory,
 for ever and ever.
Amen.

Praise

This is the day that the Lord has made;
let us rejoice in it and be glad.

FROM PSALM 118

I can say it to my family,
I can say it to my friends,
I can say it at school
– so I'll say it to you
– Good morning, God,
you're great!

Sorry

Our Father in Heaven:
Please forgive me for the things I have
    done wrong:
For bad temper and angry words;
For being greedy and wanting the best
    for myself;
For making other people unhappy:
forgive me, Heavenly Father.

DICK WILLIAMS

Help me

Dear Lord Jesus,
help me to be a friend to others today.
When they are sad, help me to comfort
    them.
When they are lonely,
help me to play with them.
When no one likes them
help me to be kind to them.
When they are frightened, help me to stay
close to them and help them to
    be brave.

MARY BATCHELOR

Our world

God of all our cities,
Each alley, street and square.
Please look down on every house
And bless the people there.

JOAN GALE THOMAS

O God, our loving Father,
thank you for the beautiful world you
have made. Remind us sometimes just
to stop and look at all the lovely things
around us. In your world even the little
everyday things are special.

MARY BATCHELOR

Birthday

Tomorrow is my birthday, Lord.
As year by year I grow;
Help me to see more clearly, Lord,
The way that I should go.
Learning to love, learning to live
Learning to use the gifts I have.
Tomorrow is my birthday, Lord,
And I'll be one year older.

FROM HELLO GOD

O Loving God, today is my birthday.
For your care from the day I was born until
today, and for your love, I thank you. Help
me to be strong and healthy, and to show
love for others, as Jesus did.

A PRAYER FROM JAPAN

Christmas

Thank you, God, for the joys of
    Christmas:
For the fun of opening Christmas
    stockings;
For Christmas trees with twinkling
    lights;
For exciting parties;
For Christmas cakes and puddings;
Thank you, God.
Thank you for all the happiness of
Christmas-time;
Thank you for the lovely presents we
    receive;
Thank you most of all that Jesus was
born as a baby on the first Christmas
    Day.
Thank you God.

Easter

Good Friday is a time of sadness,
Easter is a time of gladness.
On Good Friday Jesus died,
But rose again at Eastertide.
All thanks and praise to God.

Jesus, you're alive!
Not as you were alive in Galilee with
your friends. Then only the people
who met you could talk to you – but
now, everybody can.
Jesus, who died for me,
Help me to live for thee.

COMMUNITY OF THE GLORIOUS ASCENSION

School days

O Lord, there is such a lot to learn. Thank you that we can go to school. Some days we can't wait to go. Some days it's great to learn. Some days it's difficult or scary. Some days we don't really want to go. Help us to do our best. There is such a lot to learn in your world.

O Lord Jesus, we remember how you had lessons to learn when you were a boy. Help us to learn our lessons well. Show us how to do our best, for your sake.

More Parents' Prayers

Building a family

God our Father, bless our home and family
and teach us to live together in your love.
Help us to bring up our children in the light
of your truth so that by our care and
example they will grow up to love and
follow you.

MARION STROUD

Teaching children to pray

Lord Jesus, 'Lord teach us to pray' your
disciples once said. And you lovingly taught
them. Now I'm asked to teach my children to
pray . . . Let them think of you as someone
who knows them personally and loves them
dearly – not a frightening, mysterious, all-
seeing eye. Help them not to regard prayer as
a magic wishing well. Let them understand
that they can talk to you without following
any set form or pattern, for you are their
friend as well as their God. Let my prayers be
good examples to my children. And thank you
for all that I am learning as you teach our little
children – and me, your older child – to pray.

MARION STROUD

A bad day

Oh God, I was so cross to the children
today. Forgive me.

Oh, God, I was so discouraged, so tired.
I took it out on them. Forgive me.
Forgive me for my bad temper, my
impatience, and most of all my yelling. I
cringe to think of it. My heart aches. I want
to wake them up and beg them to forgive
me. Only I can't, it would only
upset them more.

I've got to go on living with the memory
of this day. My unjust tirades. The guilty
fear in their eyes as they flew about trying
to appease me. Thinking it all their fault —
my troubles, my disappointments. Dear
God, the utter helplessness of children.

Their vulnerability before this awful thing, adult power. And how forgiving they are, hugging me at bedtime, kissing me goodnight.

Lord, in failing these little ones whom you've put into my keeping, I'm failing you. Please let your infinite patience and goodness fill me tomorrow. Stand by me, keep your hand on my shoulder. Don't let me be so cross to my children.

MARJORIE HOLMES

Wisdom

Heavenly Father, from whom all
parenthood comes, teach us so to
understand our children that they may
grow in your wisdom and love
according to your holy will. Fill us
with sensitive respect for the great
gift of human life which you have
committed to our care, help us to
listen with patience to their worries
and problems and give us tolerance to
allow them to develop as individuals,
as your son did under the loving
guidance of Mary and Joseph.

MICHAEL BUCKLEY

Honesty

Give us the grace, Lord, to tell our
children the truth and nothing but
   the truth.
To issue no idle threats or promises.
To keep our word.
To apologize when we have been wrong.
To be disciplined over time.
To be courteous in all our dealings.
To answer children's questions as honestly
and as simply as we can.
To let them help in all the ways we
   can devise.
To expect from them no higher standard of
honesty, unselfishness, politeness than we
are prepared to live up to ourselves.

JOAN KENDALL

For ourselves

Our Father — as we shoulder the everyday responsibilities of parenthood, as we cope with the daily challenges, with tiredness and with worry, help us not to lose sight of our first joy at the birth of our baby. Help us to remember your promise to be with us and to help us, and that, when we come to you, we come to someone with a parent's heart
— our Father.

Lord make me an instrument of your
    peace;
Where there is hatred, let me sow love;
Where there is injury, pardon;
Where there is discord, union;
Where there is doubt, faith;
Where there is despair, hope;
Where there is darkness, light;
Where there is sadness, joy.

FRANCIS OF ASSISI

Our love

Lord Jesus, thank you for the business
of our days. But remind us also to take
    time out —
time for ourselves;
time to be quiet;
time to relax and to recharge our
batteries.
Bless us as we spend time with our friends
    and family.
And especially help us to spend time
with each other, listening, talking and
just being together.

Our marriage

God,
you are the source of love and you join us
together in the miracle of friendship,
    marriage and family life.
Let faithfulness, freshness and
    unselfishness
fill the deep relationships we cherish
and be a sign to the nations that this is the
    way you love the world
in Jesus Christ our Lord.

FROM FURTHER EVERYDAY PRAYERS

Letting go

Teach me to let go, Lord; to let my child
take his own steps into the big world, to
watch and care but to let him grow, as you,
Lord, let us all grow, all of us your children.
You let us make our own choices, our own
mistakes, although you love us — because
you love us. He is ours, Lord, yours and
mine; upheld by both our loves. We both
want the best for him. Let him be sure of
that, now and wherever he goes.

MORE EVERYDAY PRAYERS

Blessings

*Jesus took the children in his arms and blessed
them, laying his hands upon them.*

FROM MARK'S GOSPEL

Almighty God, look with favour on this
child; grant that, being nourished with all
goodness, he/she may grow in discipline
and grace until he/she comes to the
fullness of faith, through Jesus Christ
our Lord.

FROM THE ALTERNATIVE SERVICE BOOK 1980

God the Father, bless us;
God the Son, defend us;
God the Spirit, keep us
now and evermore.

FROM LITTLE FOLDED HANDS

The grace of the Lord Jesus Christ
and the love of God
and the fellowship of the Holy Spirit
be with us all.

FROM 2 CORINTHIANS 13

Christ be with me, Christ within me,
Christ behind me, Christ before me,
Christ beside me, Christ to win me,
Christ to comfort and restore me,
Christ beneath me, Christ above me,
Christ in quiet, Christ in danger,
Christ in mouth of friend or stranger.

PATRICK OF IRELAND

Acknowledgments

Every attempt has been made to trace copyright holders
of individual prayers. If there have been any inadvertent
omissions in the acknowledgments we apologize to those
concerned.

The Central Board of Finance of the Church of England
  for material from the Alternative Service Book 1980;
Mary Batchelor;
Kevin Mayhew Publishers for 'Heavenly Father, from whom all'
  by Michael Buckley;
Christian Publicity Organization;
From *Little Folded Hands* Copyright 1987 Concordia Publishing House.
  Used by permission;
Meryl Doney;
Hodder Headline for 'Oh God, I was so cross to the children today'
  by Marjorie Holmes Mighell, from *I've Got to Talk to Somebody, God;*
Mothers Union, for 'Give us the grace, Lord,' by Joan Kendall;
National Christian Education Council for material from
  Further Everyday Prayers and *More Everyday Prayers;*
National Society for Promoting Religious Education for material
  from *Worship in Junior Schools;*
Oxford University Press for 'May the love of God our Father' from
  Infant Prayer, edited by Margaret Kitson;
Ulrich Schaffer, *For the Love of Children*, © 1979 Ulrich Schaffer,
  Lion Publishing 1980;
Katharine Short, *A Book for Mums*, Lion Publishing 1981;
SPCK for 'Thank you for the world so sweet' by Mrs E. Rutter Leatham,
  from *Hymns and Songs for Children;*
Marion Stroud;
Kingsway Publications for 'Our Father in Heaven' by Dick Williams,
  from *Prayers for Today's Church.*